HOME and AWAY

poems by

Alan Basting

Finishing Line Press
Georgetown, Kentucky

HOME and AWAY

Copyright © 2019 by Alan Basting
ISBN 978-1-64662-014-2 First Edition
All rights reserved under International and Pan-American Copyright Conventions. No part of this book may be reproduced in any manner whatsoever without written permission from the publisher, except in the case of brief quotations embodied in critical articles and reviews.

ACKNOWLEDGMENTS

The following titles were previously published in magazines and e-journals:

"Stony Road," FUNGI Magazine; Fall 2015; also subsequently anthologized in *Mycoepithalamia: Mushroom Wedding Poems*, The FUNGI Press, 2016.
"Why We Camp," *The Birch Gang Review*; Mar/April, 2016.
"Up North Dancing," *Walloon Writers Review*, No. 2, Winter 2016.
"Faithful," *American Journal of Poetry*; Vol. 2, January 2017.
"Girl in the Woods," *Blueline*, literary journal of SUNY Pottsdam, Spring 2017.
"Local Color," *Blueline*, literary journal of SUNY Potsdam, Spring 2018.
"Ashes at the Baldwin Airport," and "Mobridge," *Common Ground Review*, literary journal of Western New England University, Fall/Winter Issue 2019.

Publisher: Leah Maines
Editor: Christen Kincaid
Cover Art: Jeff Basting
Author Photo: Cassie Basting
Cover Design: Jeff Basting

Printed in the USA on acid-free paper.
Order online: www.finishinglinepress.com
　　　also available on amazon.com

Author inquiries and mail orders:
Finishing Line Press
P. O. Box 1626
Georgetown, Kentucky 40324
U. S. A.

Table of Contents

Ashes at the Baldwin Airport 1

Fall Rituals 2

Observing a Holiday Outing 3

After 45 Years 4

Finders Keepers 5

Motorcycling to Montana 6

A Certain Mind 7

Waiting on Prodigals 9

Sitting in the Blind 10

Up North Dancing 11

Great Expectations 12

Breakfasting with Strangers 13

Tree Rats 14

Local Color 15

Why We Camp 18

Faithful 19

Girl in the Woods 21

Evangelicals 22

Stony Road 23

Forward 24

Mobridge 25

Relic 26

Speaking in Dreams 27

Assuming Frederick 28

Napping with My Grandsons 29

Hats Off to Harrison 30

*This book is dedicated to my family,
wherever you may be.*

I was joined by the head to this world.
No surgery was possible.
We keep doing things together.
—Jim Harrison, from
"After the War"

ASHES AT THE BALDWIN AIRPORT

Someone had a good idea. I saw the two of them
at the far end of a grassy runway with their urn
waving it in the wind above their heads. That could be
me in a few years, disappearing into wild grasses
and distant pines as an ashy little dust storm. Maybe it
was the family dog, the "only child" of an aging couple.
Here, because this is where he ran freely when they
walked him. The space an invitation to emptying
walks with animals. Deer and black bear occasionally
cross the distant end of the runway, then disappear
through invisible doors in scrub oak bordering
the outstretched arm of black tarmac. Big sky
everywhere, as big as I remember Dakota, riding
cycle past miles of wheat. The peaceful quiet
enormous, and welcoming as a family threshold.
Tall stalks of nodding grasses wait for someone
to say: I love how I feel in this place. Wide open.
Free as dust.

FALL RITUALS

In the middle of October a murder
of crows arrives each year for the past five.
A traveling circus, they set up performances
in surrounding oaks and willows hanging

upside down free-falling and tumbling through
branches and open air. Playing chase and tag
they squawk and banter to each other
all the while making dares. Using beak and talon

one snipped a hefty wasp's nest fifty feet
up an old maple. It fell like a chunky
brown cone straight down. As an offering
of thanks and general appreciation

for their very good show, I torch a large
pile of dry raked leaves. I think the crows
are pleased with the leafy smoke
sent out for them. Autumn incense.

OBSERVING A HOLIDAY OUTING

Straw hats, light blue shirts handmade
with denim dungarees and black suspenders;

girls in gray pleated dresses and white caps
tied beneath their chins—Mennonite children hop past

my balcony on Pogo sticks, grinning
widely, laughing happily among themselves.

Uneasy with the levity, and hopping in public,
parents switch the children to bicycles

for the return ride back to their cabins.
And, in the middle of my happy hour

margarita, I am stained
by disappointment.

AFTER 45 YEARS

Waking at 2 a.m. and wandering
the straight path to the bathroom
I peek at the moon two-thirds
across black sky overwhelmed
by light from the hard white witch.
Blanketed in her spell the Catalinas
are docile in sleep behind me.
Temperature in the 30's I just need
to make it back to the warmth
of my own covers and retreat
to the dream of what was beautiful
dark and Latina before my urges
so rudely interrupted. When I reach
the bed everyone is snoring: two
dogs and a spouse, my comfort
for years who snores louder
than both dogs. I know her volume
is higher on her back than her side
where I would like to push her.
But after 45 years of jostling
through marriage and one helluva
motorcycle accident leaving her left leg
locked and permanently straightened
who am I to deny her even one
mattress-hogging position for dreaming
and dancing with salsa-gods drumming
through her dream's miracle cure.

FINDERS KEEPERS
   —*for Jack Koch*

He signed his Christmas card, "Jack, Your Sanitation Engineer," getting a laugh out of it. He manages the township's "Transfer Station," another euphemism for what my dad called, The Dump. But Jack is round and friendly, a citizen and community historian. Fifth generation of his family birthed and buried in our obscure, horseshoe-throwing village. He digs graves for extra cash, witnesses local continuity cradle to grave, and remembers almost everything that's happened here. I told him I found a gun. A pistol, buried in the wall of my garage. He stands perfectly still for a moment, staring over my shoulder, then blinks and says, Howard, the previous owner, drank a lot. Annnd—He might have been belligerent with his wives. He had a few. Maybe one had a gun to protect herself, he says. Or maybe she hid *his* gun to protect herself? Same difference. You know, it takes time for the Barney Fife's from White Cloud to drive way up here, let alone find the address on a 9-1-1. Each of us is our own Police Department, so to speak, and I wouldn't just throw that gun away, buddy. Another thing, he says, Howard drove truck. Between the U.P. And Cleveland. Sometimes Detroit. Bad territory back then—maybe he did something with that gun, then hid it? Guess we'll never know, eh? I dug his grave after you bought that place, couple years ago. Then he laughed—belly laughed. Guess that piece is all yours now, friend. I'd be careful who I brought that up to.

MOTORCYCLING TO MONTANA

Before leaving the office my boss winks
and kids, "Just keep it between the ditches,
old timer." And while I am cruising, behaving
at the posted speed, a younger version
of myself flys by in a t-shirt, long hair
and no helmet. He roars past, wrist cranked
down on his flamed two-wheeler.
When he swings around the semi
grunting along in front of us,
he is shoved outside the berm line
by a gust's invisible hand.
The ditches on either side yawn deep
and hungry. I am suddenly grinding
my teeth, while he wrestles a bike monster
for control. But it's not happening,
and now he's into loose gravel,
pebbles shooting past like stars
flung from his plunging path.
The finish my mother always warned
would happen—
always dreaded for her eldest son.

A CERTAIN MIND

Yesterday was childhood where the sun
followed his feet across fields

of fountain grass and dwarf flax growing wild.
Maybe he counted clouds or searched them

for redeemers, his back pressed
to the ground among ants and crickets.

Their songs continue into dark
and prayers from foreign countries

where, again, the sun has found him,
wearing black, hiding under a convert's

robe, waiting with weapons drawn
for bullets and back up. The black vans

of deadly militia block the exits.
A wind flames up his face

and lifts a shadow. Orthodoxy,
its heavy wings vulture in air above him.

*

Before the final bullet arrives, his mind
a dreamy twinkle of seas, hovers

at a cliff's edge near the ocean,
where a boy, sun-drenched, peers into

white caps on the waves beneath him,
certain *this* is what his heart longs for—

a cloud's perspective. A lucid glimpse
of the cricket's lucky song

before the times of trouble
and conversion's cataract fog.

WAITING ON PRODIGALS

Are the voices of your children
drawing nearer, as adults might
pull chairs to circle a campfire

sharing stories, or is the forest
growing taller and darker
between you?

I sometimes leave
the circle of light and wander
surrounding woods, peering

into the dark rim
for an approaching candle.
And so have met others

in the night who will never
give up hoping
for that glimmer of light,

a chance to heal, square up
with beloved, addicted prodigals.
Sadly, many perish first.

SITTING IN THE BLIND

There is nothing moving except an occasional
dried leaf drifting elegantly with the breeze
through bare branches tapping the fingers

and scratching outstretched limbs of nearby oaks.
Their neighbors, the upright, straight-backed pines
stand like worthy sentinels, elected representatives

pledging allegiance to the community of northern
wood. Sun slants into west-facing columns of these
noble citizens who if they could speak might

scoff at my pathetic camouflage: What's your point,
they'd say, You look nothing like the rest of us.
Thankfully no one is speaking here besides

the runaway voices in my head. I am here
for the meat I remind myself, defensively.
So maybe it's the bloody taste then or

you can't get fresh venison from the grocery.
The ends of my feet are freezing in place
along with the tops of my hands. Wondering

about purpose only makes me colder, yet nothing
surpasses the woods: its nourishing, enveloping
quiet, captured in the Buddha's smile.

UP NORTH DANCING

Imbued with old-style self-reliance,
commemorative values and beer,
we plan to spruce up Olga.

Putting shoulders to the door
a full-blooded winter is waiting,
shaking frozen fists in our face.

Otherworldly, green belts of borealis
drift in the sky above,
luminescent playground

for the tics and moods of God.
His dark hands ask for a dance:
pines, cake-frosted, sway slowly

under eerie light from the show.
Who could resist such an invitation?
Snowshoes wobbling in circles,

hands over heads and waving,
a wolf's voice melds with our trio.

GREAT EXPECTATIONS

Anxious to complete the trek
from northern Michigan to Denver,
I am a chipper pilgrim
before an altar of coffee carafes
at Motel 6, Junction City, Kansas.

Exchanging pleasantries
with a middle-aged sunny blonde
housekeeper from town,
I mention I am hopeful
for high skies and less wind
than in the miserable passage
through Missouri, bleak and full
of rainy hills.

Sipping coffee and raising
an eyebrow, she says, "Well…
this is, after all, Kansas,"
with a small smile
wry as Mona Lisa's. "We
can wish for anything
we want, can't we."

BREAKFASTING WITH STRANGERS

Having sausage and eggs with strangers
inside "The Lodge" I am doing my damnedest
to keep from stinking it up, over-sweating, the sun

pounding in from high windows. When I look
to the lake outside the window-wall I see
a committee of vultures, fraternity brothers

perched on posts and railings surrounding
the outdoor pool, warming themselves
in morning sun and stretching huge black wings

as if yawning. Occasionally one lifts off,
cruising updrafts and scouting the neighborhood
roads and trails, scenting air for the dead or dying.

And I know where I won't be sunning
my smelly armpits this morning. But I will
make a recommendation to the high-heeled

sales priestess hustling pricey condos
near the Everglades (and smiling pythons)
among wealthy old farmers from Ohio.

TREE RATS

That's what I call them. An overabundance
of squirrels: blacks, grays and seemingly overnight
the pygmy reds whose aggression and endless appetite
only add to my distaste for them. Badgered by thoughts
that I am my own worst enemy in the battle
for control of my feeder, I am crossed between impulses:
withhold food, denying even my favorite
grosbeaks, cardinals and finches, or continue priming
gluttony among the short-hairs with question-mark tails.
With how much karmic wrath would I paint myself
by blasting them off my feeder? Only Kali, the dark
Goddess of Time, holds the secret and continues dancing.
Staring out the window and watching a fat gray
devour fistfuls of flavored suet meant for chickadees,
nuthatches and our beloved pileated woodpecker, my blood
heats up. I bang the door open to frighten him off:
nothing doing. I shout and stomp my feet. Nothing doing.
Forgetting I was on my way to the shower I hurry
back to my room and grab the shotgun. The last thing
this gluttonous hairball sees is a naked fool
in black felt slippers shouldering a metallic stick
pointed in his direction.

LOCAL COLOR

Lacking the loon's elegance
and its ability to dive deep

for food, this one hops...one-legged
among his red-winged brethren.

Shouldering his way, he jabs
his beak, rummages through husks

for a seed-bit nugget. (Steak
and caramelized suet?

Not on the menu.) No crutch,
No Special Olympics,

He survives... in a world where
shark-eyed jays & omnivorous starlings

wait for him to weaken:
He can fly, he can fly, but

he knows he must sleep
and feed among friends.

*

Spreading dangling arms
along banks of clear creeks

rippled with sandy bottoms
and shorelines of iron-tinged lakes,

loosestrife advances, its gnarled
rhizomeic persistence, a slow suffocation

for diversity in wetland plant life.
Invasive woodland baron, the weed

is closing down the feeder stream,
choking the lake's little engine.

When its work in the stream is finished,
it will bury the lake creating

a marshland of root balls, woody stems
and flowering pink seed pods

attractive to beaver, birds and insects
who feast and spread the reach

of strangling loosestrife. Without
judgment the sun bestows this

flourishing repast, unwittingly
called the butterfly plant.

    *

Without judgment the moon's
bright indifference provides diamonds

and stars glinting up nightly
from the creek's smooth surface—

there for everyone,
including the tanned molester

who wonders why no one
will love him, his impatient hands,

chains tattooed around his wrists.
His trailer's an ugly stump

among A-framed woodsy gardeners
who thrive on corporate income.

    *

Pushing back wet cold
from his shoulders, the blackbird

shudders under a cape
of night's rain. Sunrise

lighting tips of neighboring pines
reminds him

it's almost time for breakfast. Time
to find some friends.

Daylilies, tiger-orange and brown,
erupt along the creek sides,

painting the stream beneath them,
a spillage of orange-petaled lava.

WHY WE CAMP

Between the grease
of thumb & forefinger,

a relief map
held the compassed lives

of hikers, their legend
and happy past.

In the flimflam light
of a smiling moon,

an insect sang
of God's dependable hand,

the Southern Cross,
a virgin's ripening womb,

until his guitar
was quietly stolen.

Once cold and uninvested,
a girl who sang in the choir

blossomed for the wild mountains
filling with deer, who waited

in quelled and fading light
before descending

to the lake's edge for a drink
and the solace

of star-covered waters,
a peace that each could swallow.

FAITHFUL

In case of emergency
Call _____,

a ghost of a woman
not picking up her cell,

unreachable, walking away,
a Levi's jacket thrown over

her shoulder, the smell of fried
chicken and bar smoke

embedded in fabric
wafting from her shirttails.

Oh friend, how
could I have come

to depend on one
so free, so attached

to a lunchbox of mishaps,
a ponytail, and a family

who loved their bourbon
with eclairs.

    *

Jumbled by stroke
and its smoky plume

I see her struggle with confusion,
a stage full of purple light

and fog. Not knowing
where her body stops,

where memory begins,
she falls constantly, relearning

to read and write, to speak
again with her friends.

*

Sitting in a courtyard
landscaped with red umbrellas,

she taps the tree of sorrow,
singing blues again with the dead.

A knife, handle erect
in a clay pot's soil, broadcasts

the fragrance of microphones
from a fistful of yellow roses.

*

The door might be locked,
the fountains barely gurgling,

but I maintain my faith in her
fading symptoms, her cure

impending for months,
maybe years.

GIRL IN THE WOODS

Wading through a puddle of crows
amok with the grammar of love,

she throws crusts to the bluest ones
who speak to her with eyes.

Suspicious. The way deer are
beguiled with the taste of carrots

and apples, set out as offerings
or bait. Their deaths imagined for them

by a woman, up early in darkness,
sitting quietly behind a blind.

Later, there will be blood and
hot coffee spilled in snow.

A mixed toast to a morning full
of gunshots and squawking crows.

EVANGELICALS

I built a house where clouds were swept,
puffy bison stampeding
the hard blue skies over our lake,

a choppy dither beneath them.
I watched the wind, its violent indifference,
thinking time will come for us,

a distant whistler cresting hills,
mucking through swamp and valley
to extend its withering hand,

the heart's weather chilled
from swallowing morsels of frost.
Reduced from an earthquake, faith

holds hands when weather turns
wind and rain against us. Still
we must find love's sweetness—

the berry vines and wild seeds
tucked among twiggy thickets, feeding
orioles, warblers and wrens,

finch-sized missionaries,
carrying love's message in song.

STONY ROAD

I sat by the road before the storm
hit, nursing on a pair of gloves, broken

and dreaming, the wealth of maples
crowded in the air above me.

And below, dirt and shade of the street,
full of noise and a black-robed woman

with a black umbrella, who turned
and walked toward Law offices, aromas

of roasting ox. In her prayers: chickens,
a reverence for all things

slain for our stomachs, and mercy
as we devour His creatures.

Give us thy daily bread, oh Lord, and
a mushroom to protect us

from our instincts, hidden like leg traps
on home's stony road before us.

FORWARD

Resting my eyes, disconnected,
I merge with a dream
in the nap of a snoozy magpie
dozing in a juniper in north
New Mexico, over a valley floor
of grasses gold and dry. Sloping up
and away, a range of shadowy mountains,
old volcanoes, table tops for the dice
of gods, and above them a sapphire sky
traveled by billowy clouds, ghosts
of drifting bison. Long black tracks
of the railroad stretch east from a furnace
orange western horizon. Across this valley
a train pulled by four diesels rolls,
calm as deep river current, with two
hundred box cars behind. And I find
my mind in those engines, calm and
determined, hauling the freight of my life
from sunset to a darkening east,
at peace, pulling toward night
and the spangle of brilliant stars,
cradled in the thrum of diesels
rumbling through my sleep.

MOBRIDGE

Time to go back to Mobridge. I left
in a hurry and I need to undo it. There's
a promontory west of the city crowned
by the granite likeness of Sitting Bull.
He stares out, unhappily, shot to death
by government Indians, agency police
who feared him and the rising power
of the Ghost Dance. From the overlook
he can see south down the Missouri, winding
past distant bluffs and valley ranches,
weather blown to him from western skies,
the cloud spirits dancing and thundering
before him. I sat on the stone steps
leading to his bones, and I, too, watched
a storm roll up the valley, tossing down
great spears of lightning. Suddenly I felt him
at my back. A dream-thief intruder caught
in the act, I had sensations, like ones I had
as a child at the top of the stairs (a darkened
room behind me) panicking and running
down, escaping grisly hands reaching
for my neck from the darkness. I jumped
from his steps, threw a leg over my cycle,
and sped away, my fear following
like a snake's tail. Now I want to go back.
Face the dark feelings. Say, I know why
you wanted me gone, my cultural whiteness
offensive to the spiritual landscape, where
at least your bones have peace. Say,
my apologies for the intrusion.

RELIC

It wasn't what I was expecting, traveling
open range through northwest South Dakota,
2003. Winter wheat rolled in swells
of prairie ocean. Detuned and relaxed
from the cushion of an old Goldwing,
my eyes scrolled miles of planted fields
to the horizon where the two lanes
disappeared, a peaceful, stretching dream.
Then, on the crest of a hill positioned
out near the highway where no one
could miss it, a huge, rolled bale of hay
drying in wind and sun. On top, anchored
carefully in the straw hair, an American flag
fluttering for all it was worth. A bold,
bare-chested statement. And this on lands
belonging to Lakota. As an aging hippie
I remembered thinking how out of step I felt
with whatever was "happening" in this country.
Yesterday, I flashbacked to the feeling,
witnessing a date between teens
sitting next to each other for coffee
and conversing— over their phones.

SPEAKING IN DREAMS

My friend, hemmed in by losses
and a pounding from the years,

is mapped with wrinkles.
Carpenter by trade he shows us

his hands, tree roots wrapped
in hardening skin.

These fingers once held
a piece of the sky, he says,

but there was a woman I met
who held me.

*

At the house with two lamps
and a broken mirror, my deceased

father waits, wearing a ball cap
and his favorite, old robe. He speaks

like Jesus, in parables:
There is no room in heaven

large enough for a man
crowded with desires, he says,

looking me right in the eye,
shrugging, turning both palms up.

*

Sitting upright in bed, staring
into darkness, I hug my pillow

and do not speak.

ASSUMING FREDERICK
—*for my father*

The inheritance wasn't what I expected,
or wanted, but some things can't be
waived or bumped off projected paths,
like the shape of my skull, for instance,

the bald, flat area at the back. Or growing
jowls with age, even as I lose weight. Worse,
a look darts from my eyes (maybe
his eyes) as I step away from mirrors,

glancing at the shape of me leaving,
thinking, *Yes, I see what you are seeing,
shadows in your face, like his.* I hear
his voice when I suddenly call out

warnings to my four-year old grandson—
or in the sounds I make when sipping soup
or coffee. I can put up with the pot belly,
since now I know where it comes from,

a reminder I am slowing down,
getting older, easier for his shape
and presence to mold me. Then what?
A voice in my head says, *Hey, you could do worse...*

NAPPING WITH MY GRANDSONS

With my neck bent,
head bowed,
chin resting
on the thumbprint of my heart,

I am listening
to their breath
and my heart's drum,
summoning the stars to dance.

On a midnight beach
with the peach scent
of blossoms wafting,
our feet begin

a Cha-cha. Gone the worry
over Christmas eviction,
the shadowy noose of father's
addiction. Gone the fear

and wild confusion
during kindergarten drills
for an *active shooter*.
Our footsteps swing

to a polka, laughing stars
whirl on the dance floor
above. Outstretched hands
stirring the air around us,

we are a cartoon
of happy movement.

HATS OFF TO HARRISON: AN ADAPTATION FROM GHAZAL #1
—for drummer, Robert Thompson

We need to get back before the music begins, planetary,
pixelated, wind-scattered, waiting to be drawn together

by the drum. Dark green voices and dancers listening,
birds, crickets and ocean waves, a glazed hysteria

among the soon-to-be-blessed. Let us have tambourine, sax,
guitars and forests, fruits, and a new constellation to guide us,

a holy book in the hands of the drummer, rock steady
behind his kit, driving this musical big rig down the road,

a cosmic highway of night and stars. I saw him, the drummer.
He was jamming, and smiling as he passed through our village.

Alan Basting was born in Detroit in 1949. He graduated in 1967 from Maumee High School in northwest Ohio. He attended Earlham College and received his undergraduate degree from University of Cincinnati. Later he earned graduate degrees from Colorado State University and Bowling Green State University. He taught writing and literature at the University of Cincinnati and Owens Community College in Toledo. His chapbooks include *Singing from the Abdomen,* Stone-Marrow Press; *What the Barns Breathe,* Windows Press; *Suddenly, Herons,* The Writers' Cooperative of Toledo; and *Deep Time, Daily Habits and Events,* from The Arts Commission of Toledo, Ohio. His collection, *Nothing Very Sudden Happens Here,* was published by Lynx House Press, Spokane, WA, in late 2013. Poems for the new chapbook, *Home and Away,* have appeared in *The American Journal of Poetry; Birch Gang Review; Walloon Writers Review; Fungi Magazine; Blueline,* and *Common Ground Review.* Most of the year, he lives in the middle of the Manistee National Forest near the village of Bitely, MI, with his spouse and two dogs. More of Alan's story and poetry from nearly all of his chapbooks can be found at www.alanbastingpoetry.com Please visit him there.

www.ingramcontent.com/pod-product-compliance
Lightning Source LLC
LaVergne TN
LVHW041601070426
835507LV00011B/1233